DIAGNOSTIC INTRATHORACIC TUBERCULOSIS IN CHILDREN

A Guide For Low Income Countries
2003

Robert Gie

International Union Against Tuberculosis and Lung Disease
68 Boulevard Saint-Michel, 75006 Paris, France

This publication was made possible in part through support provided by the United States Agency for International Development under the terms of Award No. HRN-a-00-00-00018-00. The opinions expressed herein are those of the author(s) and do not necessarily reflect the views of the United States Agency for International Development.

This publication was made possible in part through support provided by the United States Centers for Disease Control and Prevention.

PREFACE

Tuberculosis (TB) remains one of the greatest health problems for people living in the developing world. The diagnosis, treatment, and management of tuberculosis in adults have been well-documented and tested in most parts of the world. In adults the problem is primarily that of access to medical services.

For children the problems are much greater. In most national tuberculosis programmes, children are not a priority, and, even in those programmes that cater to children, diagnosis is difficult, resulting in a large number of cases that are incorrectly managed. Either children with chronic chest diseases are unnecessarily treated for tuberculosis, or the diagnosis is made so late that the children die from their tuberculosis or have severe lung damage due to it.

The diagnosis of childhood intrathoracic tuberculosis depends on a constellation of symptoms, signs, and tuberculin skin test and chest radiograph findings. As a result, making a diagnosis is fraught with difficulty.

The goal of this illustrated atlas of intrathoracic tuberculosis in children is to assist health care workers practicing in low-income countries in the interpretation of the chest radiograph in children suspected of having TB. It is not meant to replace the radiologist's or specialist's opinion, but rather should be used as an aid for health care workers in hospitals where there is limited access to a radiologist or specialist.

Many of us who have traveled and taught in the developing world realize that access to chest radiographs is difficult, but getting them interpreted can be even more problematic. I therefore hope that, by giving examples of common radiological pictures of intrathoracic tuberculosis, the diagnosis of childhood TB will be improved.

Acknowledgements

I would especially like to acknowledge the following:

Prof. Donald Enarson and Penny Enarson from the International Union Against Tuberculosis and Lung Disease and Prof. Nulda Beyers from the IUATLD Childhood Tuberculosis Working Group for encouragement and support with the project. My colleagues Drs. Sharon Kling, Pierre Goussard and Simon Schaaf who helped me collect the cases; Prof. JA Beyers who stimulated my interest in the subject, and the many students who have encouraged me.

The following persons are gratefully acknowledged for reviewing this guide: Drs. Magda Makram (Sudan), Charles Mwasambo (Malawi), Steve Graham (Malawi) and Jeff Starke (USA).

Robert Gie
Department of Paediatrics and Child Health
Universiteit Stellenbosch
South Africa

2003

CONTENTS

I. INTRODUCTION

With the increasing interest in childhood tuberculosis (TB) the difficulties in making the diagnosis of intrathoracic TB are becoming increasingly clear. In adults suspected of having tuberculosis, the diagnosis in the majority of cases is confirmed by examination of the sputum for acid-fast bacilli. In adults chest radiography plays a small part in the diagnosis of TB. However, due to the paucibacillary nature of TB infection and disease in children, the diagnosis in the minority of these cases is based on bacteriology. Generally, diagnosis is made from a combination of history, tuberculin skin test, and the chest radiograph. The chest radiograph is one of one of the most commonly used tests in the diagnosis of TB, but it has its own inherent problems, as there is a large intra- and inter-observer variability in interpretation of the radiograph.

The goal of this book is to help clinicians improve their skills in reading chest radiographs of children suspected of having intrathoracic TB. It is not a complete atlas of all the possible radiological pictures of TB in children, but rather a simplified approach to the common pictures. To make the diagnosis, the clinician must integrate both the clinical and radiological pictures.

The target audience of this atlas is health care workers who are looking after children in district hospitals where chest radiographs are available, as well as those workers in national TB programmes who have to evaluate children in contact with newly diagnosed adult cases, or referred children who are thought to be suffering from TB.
The book is organized to help the reader recognize the common epidemiological, pathophysiological, and clinical aspects of childhood TB and to use these to aid in the diagnosis of childhood TB. The radiological atlas is arranged from the common uncomplicated picture to more complicated forms of intrathoracic TB in childhood.

Recognizing more complicated forms of intrathoracic childhood TB is becoming more important as HIV becomes more common, and clinical and radiological pictures are being seen which are easily and often confused with TB in HIV-infected children.

II. DIFFICULTIES IN THE DIAGNOSIS OF TUBERCULOSIS IN CHILDHOOD

Due to the fact that most childhood TB is paucibacillary, the sputum is usually smear negative, with a positive culture in only a minority of cases. In the majority of cases, the diagnosis is made based on the history of contact with an adult smear- positive case, the symptoms and signs of chronic infection, and the special investigations that include tuberculin skin testing and chest radiography. All of these have their own inherent problems:

1.   **Contact with an adult index case,** especially if the case is sputum smear positive, makes infection with TB highly likely.

      While this is nearly always the case for children living in low-burden countries, it is not always true for children living in high-burden countries. Children younger than two years of age are more likely to be infected in the household by their parents or caregivers, while children older than two years are more likely to be infected in the community. For children living in high-burden countries, the absence of a household contact certainly does not exclude the likelihood of TB.

2.   **The symptoms and signs** are very vague and common to symptoms and signs seen in children with other chronic diseases or infections, especially HIV infection. This is particularly true for symptoms commonly used in the diagnosis of TB, such as chronic cough, weight loss, fever lasting many days, and repeated respiratory tract infections.

3.   **Tuberculin skin tests** identify children infected with TB, but not necessarily those with active disease. The test can be positive in children who are asymptomatic (TB infection), as well as those with disease (TB disease). False-negative tests can occur in children with severe malnutrition after measles and other severe infections, including HIV all conditions commonly found in high-burden countries.

4. **Chest radiographs** are difficult to interpret, with great intra- and inter-observer variability reported. Often in low-income countries, facilities for chest radiographs are developed for adults, and radiographers are not readily available. This can lead to poor quality chest radiographs that are difficult or impossible to evaluate.

5. **Culture of *M. tuberculosis*** is expensive, has a low yield, and is not available in most low-income countries. In the best circumstances, the highest yields are about 40 percent.

6. Due to the fact that the diagnosis is difficult, various **scoring systems and diagnostic algorithms** have been developed. Many of these systems have not been tested. Those that have been tested in low-income countries with a high prevalence of both TB and HIV are very insensitive and non-specific for the diagnosis of TB. New scoring systems need to be developed.

It should be clear, therefore, that the clinician must have a high level of suspicion that a child has TB, and then use all the tests to make the best diagnosis possible, however imperfect it might be.

III. PATHOGENESIS OF TUBERCULOSIS IN CHILDREN AS RELATED TO THE DIAGNOSIS

Tuberculosis infection follows inhalation of *Mycobacterium tuberculosis* in a 3-5 μ m particle. The particles settle in the alveoli where single or multiple foci proliferate (primary focus) and then spread via the lymphatic system to the nearest hilar lymph glands (primary complex) (Ghon complex). The primary focus can occur in any of the lobes of the lung as particle deposition is determined by the distribution of ventilation. A patient can also have more than one primary focus. In most cases, the infection is contained at this stage and the children do not develop disease. The primary complex can often be seen on a chest radiograph as a calcified nodule in the lung and lymph glands in the mediastinum.

In children in whom the disease is contained, hypersensitivity to tuberculoprotein develops. This is demonstrated by the development of a positive tuberculin (Mantoux) skin test.

In other children, the infection continues to proliferate. The hilar lymph glands enlarge and can be seen on chest radiography. Further progression leads to involvement of the adjacent bronchus. The radiological picture of childhood TB is the result of the primary focus and complications caused by the enlarged mediastinal lymph glands. The degree of involvement of the bronchus by the lymph glands leads to a wide variation in the radiological pictures. The lymph gland can partially obstruct the bronchus, creating a "check valve" effect leading to a hyper-inflated lobe or lung; or it can completely obstruct the bronchus, leading to collapse of a lobe or segment of the lobe. These forms are termed lymphobronchial TB.

In about 10% of cases, the alveolar infiltration breaks through to the pleural space, which provokes a hypersensitivity response in the pleura and a large pleural effusion. The inflammatory response in the pleura is characterized by granulomas in which lymphocytes predominate. This finding is used in the diagnosis of tuberculous pleural effusions, as the effusions are rich in lymphocytes.

The alveolar lesion (primary focus) can also continue to enlarge. If the lesion enlarges sufficiently, central necrosis develops, and this can lead to cavitation. Cavities do occur in children, but are uncommon.

In some children, especially the young, the infection is not contained. Haematogenous dissemination of the organisms occurs and spreads the organisms throughout the body, leading to acute disseminated TB (miliary TB).

Age and immune status also play an important role in determining the clinical and radiological pictures of childhood TB. Young infants do not contain the infection well, and therefore have a higher incidence of miliary TB. These young children also have more compliant airways, which are more easily compressed by the mediastinal lymph glands. Young children and immune-suppressed children develop complicated and unusual forms of intrathoracic TB due to altered immune responses to *Mycobacterium tuberculosis*.

Children in their teens more frequently develop pleural effusions and chronic pulmonary TB (post-primary TB), which is characterized by alveolar infiltration and the formation of cavities in the upper lobes. In these children, the same strategies are used to diagnose TB as in adults, since the type of TB is similar.

IV. BASICS OF THE CHEST RADIOGRAPH INTERPRETATION

Chest radiography is the cornerstone of the diagnosis of intrathoracic tuberculosis. The great danger is that the chest radiograph is seen in isolation, without taking into account the clinical history, examination. and tuberculin skin test. A balanced view is needed to ensure that there is not over- or under-diagnosis.

The following basic conditions must be met:
1. Full-size chest radiographs must be taken. If possible, a lateral chest radiograph should also be taken, as this increases the diagnostic yield in childhood TB.

2. All previous chest radiographs should be available for accurate interpretation.

3. A good viewing box makes the examination easier.

4. The chest radiograph should be examined in a systematic manner.

Basic approach to the chest radiograph (Figs. 1, 2):
1. First check the **identity** of the patient and the date of the chest radiograph.

2. Now look at *three* aspects concerning the **quality** of the chest radiograph:
    a) Rotation
    Check rotation by looking at the clavicle head ends or by ensuring that the rib ends are equidistant from the chest edge. The position of the patient is also important as lordotic views are difficult to evaluate.
    b) Penetration
    Correct penetration is ensured when the intervertebral spaces can just be distinguished through the heart shadow.

    c) Inspiration
    Adequate inspiration is when the $8^{th}9^{th}$ posterior rib, or the 6th anterior rib, is visible.

The next step is to look at the *three* structures that are **white**:

3. a) Soft tissue

Examine the soft tissue of the chest for swelling or lumps.

b) Bony structures

Examine the bony tissue for fractures, signs of rickets or areas of infiltration.

c) Heart shadow

Examine the cardiac shadow for position, size and shape.

The next step is to look at the *three* structures that are **black**:

4. a) The trachea and the bronchi

Follow the trachea and bronchi carefully, looking for displacement or narrowing.

b) The right and left lung

c) Stomach bell

Look to ensure that the gas shadow in the stomach does not extend into the chest (hernia).

When looking at the **lung** always follow these *three* steps:

5. a) Compare the sizes of the two lungs.

b) Compare the vascularity of the two lungs.

c) Compare the two hilar shadows for:

i. Position

ii. Size

iii Shape

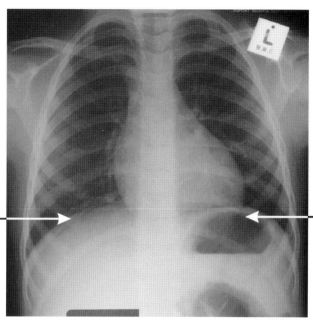

Figure 1. Normal chest radiograph. Note the good inspiration, lack of rotation, and good penetration. The rib ends are marked to aid in evaluating absence of rotation.

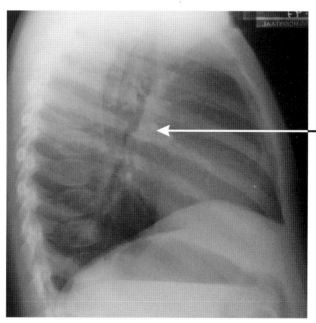

Figure 2. The normal lateral chest radiograph. It is common to mistake the normal pulmonary artery for enlarged lymph glands (see arrow).

6. Check three aspects of the diaphragm and pleura:
    a) The position of the left and right diaphragms
    b) The two costophrenic angles
    c) The pleura on both sides

Quality Features

Rotation is absent when the clavicle ends are equidistant from the midline. This is often difficult to see in small children. A useful technique is to measure the rib ends projecting over the lung fields and compare the two sides, which should be similar (Fig. 1). **Inspiration** is adequate if $8^{th}9^{th}$ posterior ribs or 6th anterior ribs are visible. In young children, counting the posterior ribs is more accurate as their ribs are more horizontal, making counting anterior ribs inaccurate. **Penetration** is adequate if the intervertebral spaces are just visible through the heart shadow. Ensure that the radiographs are not lordotic as this can make interpretation difficult.

One of the normal structures that often causes considerable difficulty in deciding if the mediastinum is wider than usual and therefore containing enlarged lymph glandsis the thymic shadow in a young child. The thymus is normally not visible in children older than four years. The classic sign of the thymic shadow is the sail sign (Fig. 3).

It is important to ensure that the chest radiograph is of acceptable quality, as a poor quality chest radiograph can lead to an incorrect diagnosis. Included is an example of a chest radiograph of unacceptable quality (Fig. 4).

**Good quality chest radiographs are needed.
A systematic approach to reading is required.**

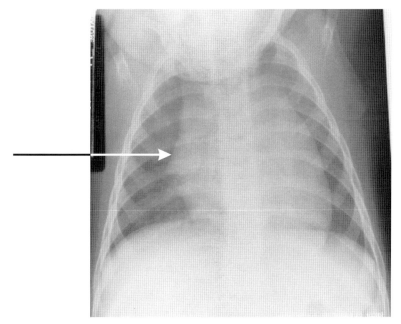

Figure 3. Common cause for a widened mediastinum in a young child is a large thymus which causes the sail sign on the chest radiograph (see arrow).

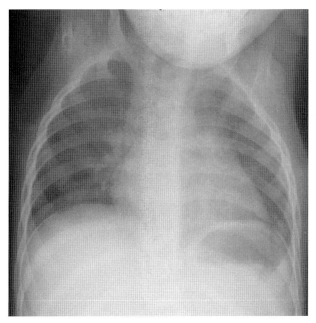

Figure 4. This is a poor-quality chest radiograph. The radiograph is of insufficient penetration, of poor inspiration, and is rotated, leading to the possible misinterpretation of hilar lymph glands.

V. UNCOMPLICATED PRIMARY DISEASE

Uncomplicated primary tuberculosis is the most common form of TB seen in clinics. The radiological picture is that of a primary focus in the lung with accompanying mediastinal lymph gland enlargement.

Complete primary complex
The primary focus is often so small that it is most often not visible and only the accompanying mediastinal lymph gland enlargement is seen. The primary focus can occur in any of the lobes and is not limited to the upper lobes, as in adults. Although the primary focus has no preference for any lobe, it tends to occur 1-2 cm from the pleura. It is normally poorly circumscribed and is less than 1 cm in diameter.

Primary complex with only mediastinal lymph gland enlargement visible
The mediastinal lymph gland enlargement is most commonly seen in the hilar regions of the lung (Fig. 5). The lymph gland enlargement is usually unilateral, but bilateral lymph gland enlargement does occur.

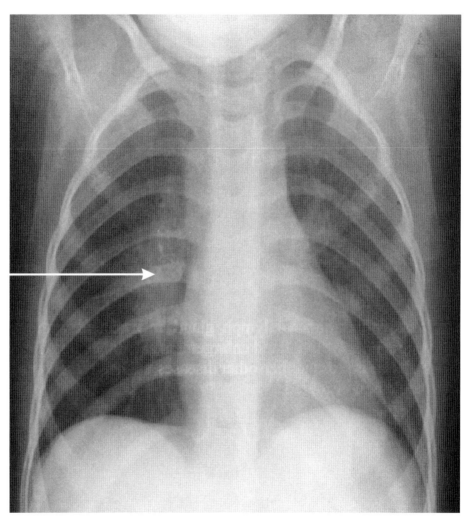

Figure 5. Uncomplicated hilar lymph gland enlargement on the right-hand side. The Ghon focus is not visible. Arrow indicates typical hilar lymph gland enlargement.

It is common to see the enlarged glands with infiltration into the surrounding lung tissue (Fig. 6). Visible hilar and paratracheal lymph gland enlargement occurs, but is less common.

Massive paratracheal lymph gland enlargement without visible hilar lymph gland enlargement seldom occurs (Fig. 7). If this is present, then other diseases, such as lymphoma, should be considered.

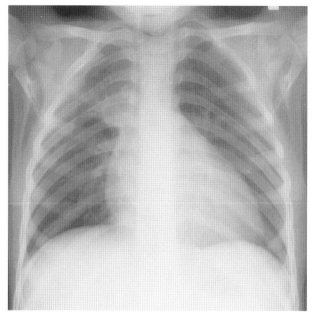

Figure 6. Hilar lymph gland enlargement with infiltration into the surrounding lung tissue.

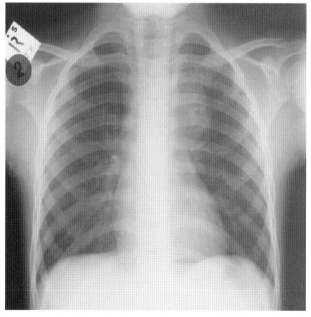

Figure 7. Left paratracheal lymph gland enlargement visible on this chest radiograph seldom occurs in isolation in tuberculosis. It is usually accompanied by hilar lymph gland enlargement.

A lateral chest radiograph is often useful in helping to visualize the hilar lymph gland enlargement. Care must be taken not to confuse the main pulmonary arteries with hilar lymph gland enlargement (see Fig. 2), but if the area designated by the arrow has well-circumscribed round lesions present, then lymph gland enlargement is certainly present (Figs. 8, 9).

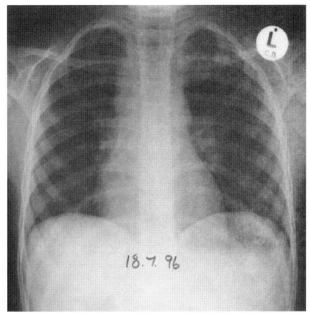

Figure 8. Suspected hilar and paratracheal lymph gland enlargement. The diagnosis can be made with more certainty when a lateral chest radiograph is examined as well (Fig. 9).

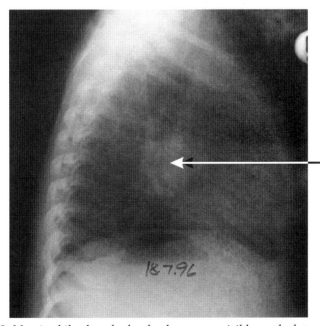

Figure 9. Massive hilar lymph gland enlargement visible on the lateral chest radiograph. The arrow indicates the hilar lymph glands.

Primary complex with mediastinal lymph gland enlargement not visible

Often the hilar lymph gland enlargement is not clearly visible or distinguishable from the pulmonary vessels. In this case, careful evaluation of the airways is often helpful, as compression of the airways especially the right and left main bronchi is indirect evidence of hilar lymph gland enlargement. A more penetrated chest radiograph is often useful for visualizing the airways (Figs. 10 and 13).

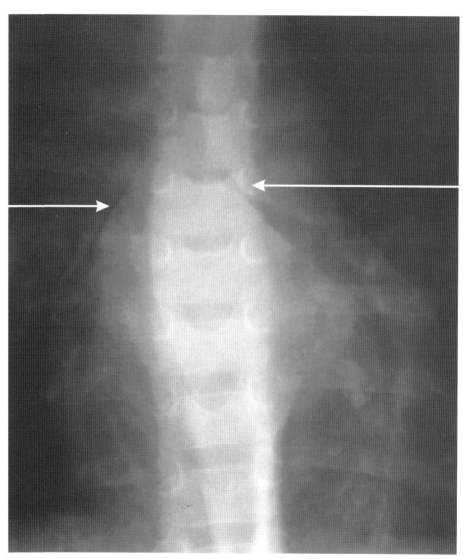

Figure 10. Often the glands are only indirectly visible by their compression of the large airways (see arrows). Large subcarinal glands are also visible.

Airway compression due to lymph gland enlargement is more common in younger infants. Other causes of airway compression occur, such as bronchogenic cysts or vascular anomalies, but, in areas of high TB prevalence, TB lymph gland enlargement is the most common. In a minority of cases, the diagnosis is enabled by observing a calcified Ghon focus (Fig. 11). Uncomplicated primary infection can pass unnoticed, with calcified glands becoming visible on chest radiographs taken later for other reasons (Fig. 12).

> **Hilar lymph gland enlargement is often seen by its compression of airways.**

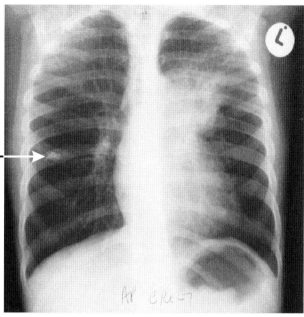

Figure 11. In a minority of cases, the diagnosis is simplified by the presence of a previous Ghon focus, which is calcified (see arrow). Mediastinal lymph gland enlargement with lung infiltration is seen on the left

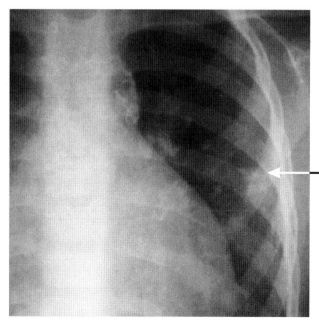

Figure 12. Calcifications occur a year after the infection. In this case, the calcified Ghon complex is a useful indicator of where the hilar and paratracheal glands are situated.

VI. COMPLICATED PRIMARY PULMONARY DISEASE

Understanding the pathogenesis of primary disease makes interpreting the radiographs of complicated primary disease easier. Complicated disease follows the involvement of the infected lymph nodes and the adjacent large airways, mainly the bronchi. As the airways become more involved, the airway lumen decreases. As the lumen narrows or the gland ulcerates into the airway, the clinical and radiological picture of the child changes. These forms of TB are called **lymphobronchial TB.**

1. **Large airway obstruction**

   Occasionally the involved glands obstruct the bronchi, causing a clinical picture that is often confused with asthma. Clinically, the diagnosis is suspected as the airway obstruction responds poorly to bronchodilators. Obstruction of the bronchi is normally accompanied by visible glands in the mediastinum; but, in younger patients, the obstruction is only visible by following the trachea and bronchi. Narrowing of the major airways can then be seen (Fig. 13). In most cases, the obstruction clears on medical treatment.

2. **Unilateral hyperinflation**

   This is not a common radiological picture. As the airways start to narrow, a point is reached where the narrowing acts as a "check valve", allowing air to be trapped in the affected lobe or lung (Fig. 14). The diagnosis is best made by combining the clinical examination with the radiological picture. On clinical examination, the affected lung is hyperinflated, with decreased air entry on auscultation.

   The radiological picture is that of a hyperinflated enlarged lung or lobe with decreased vascularity. In some cases, the glands are not directly visible, but compression of the airways can be seen. The most common cause of unilateral hyperinflation is foreign body aspiration.

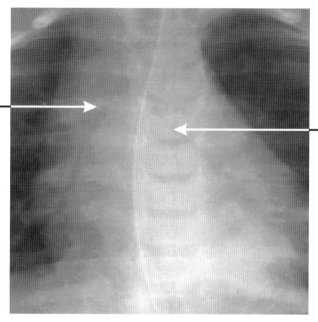

Figure 13. Compression of both the left and right main bronchi (see arrow). This child has severe airway obstruction.

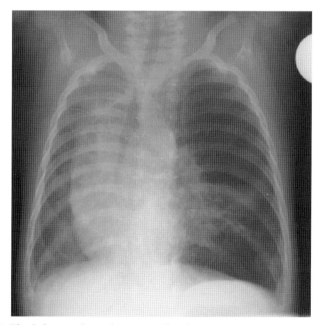

Figure 14. The left main bronchus partially obstructed, acting as a "check valve" leading to hyperinflation of the left lung.

TB expansile pneumonia

3. With complete occlusion of the airways, a number of different clinical and radiological pictures occur. When the lymph node ulcerates through the bronchus wall, it causes occlusion of the bronchus as well as aspiration of infected material into the lobe. Continued immunological response in the lobe leads to the accumulation of infected material in the lobe. This process leads to expansion in the size of the lobe. The increase in size of the lobe is seen by upward or downward displacement of the fissures.

The radiological picture is that of a densely consolidated lobe or lung without any visible air bronchograms. The fissure is displaced and the size of the lobe increased (Fig. 15). This is best seen on the lateral chest radiograph. The lymph nodes are seldom seen as they are hidden by the opacified lobe, but airway compression is common. The expansile process can be so vigorous that the mediastinum can be displaced to the opposite side (Figs. 15 and 20). As the process proceeds, necrosis of the lobe occurs, and cavities are commonly seen (Fig. 16). When the left upper lobe is involved, it is often accompanied by phrenic nerve palsy.

These lesions recover to a large degree on treatment, but result in a small fibrotic lobe. In a minority of patients, this type of lesion leads to bronchiectasis of the lobe (see Fig. 35).

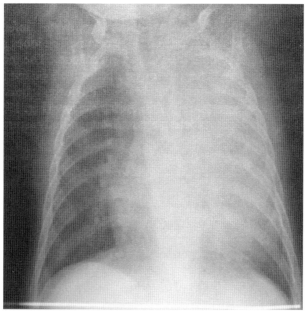

Figure 15. Expansile pneumonia of the left upper lobe with compression of the left main bronchus and displacement of the trachea and mediastinum to the right.

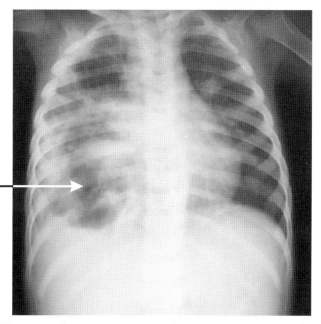

Figure 16. The expansile pneumonia can undergo extensive necrosis leading to large and multiple cavities as seen in the right middle and lower lobes.

Lobar or segmental collapse

4. With complete obstruction of the airways by the infected lymph gland, collapse of the segment or lobe occurs. The lobes affected are usually the right middle lobe or the lower lobes. The most difficult collapse to observe is the left lower lobe, as the lobe remains hidden behind the cardiac shadow. The collapsed left lower lobe is visible as a double shadow seen through the cardiac shadow (Fig. 17). Common causes of collapse are mucus plugs and foreign-body aspiration.

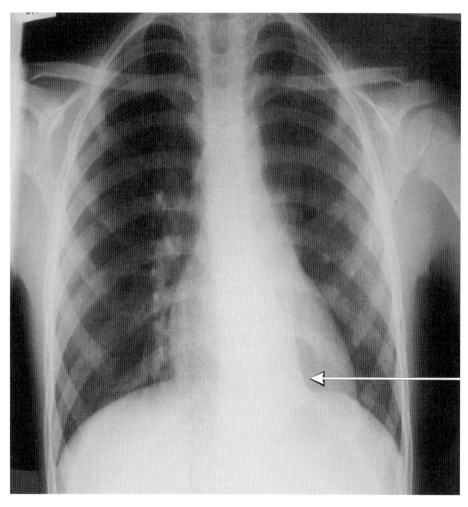

Figure 17. Left lower lobe collapse with the double shadow seen through the cardiac shadow. The left main bronchus can in some cases be seen running down at a more acute angle, not seen in this radiograph.

5. **Tuberculous bronchopneumonia**
   With ulceration of the lymph nodes through the bronchus wall, aspiration of tuberculous material can occur throughout the lung, leading to bronchopneumonia. This clinical picture most often occurs in young children who are acutely ill, and they often require supplementary oxygen. Another mechanism that can lead to TB bronchopneumonia is aspiration of material from cavitating lesions (Fig. 18).

6. **Combination of the above complications**
   Some children develop a combination of the lesions above, or they may combine these with other radiological pictures like miliary TB or pleural effusions (Fig. 19).

7. **Unrecognizable radiological patterns**
   In a minority of cases, the pathogenesis and chest radiograph pictures are impossible to explain. It is often only while at follow-up that the underlying pathology becomes clear.

Complicated primary disease is the result of lymph nodes narrowing, obstructing, or ulcerating into airways.

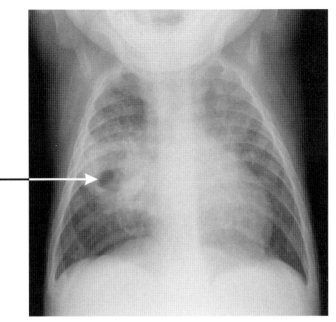

Figure 18. Cavity in the right middle lobe resulting in the spread of the TB to the rest of the lung, giving a bronchopneumonic radiological picture.

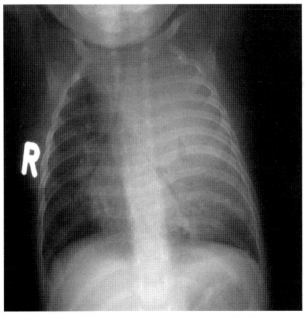

Figure 19. A combination of features is sometimes seen. In the case above, there is expansile pneumonia with a cavity in the left upper lobe, and compression of the left main bronchus and trachea with bronchopneumonia of the right upper lobe.

VII. PLEURAL DISEASE

As adolescence approaches, the number of children presenting with large pleural effusions increases. These pleural effusions are the result of a hypersensitive immune response to the tuberculoprotein in the pleural cavity. They occur when the primary focus ruptures into the pleura cavity, releasing the tuberculoprotein and a small number of bacilli.

Children normally present with fever and an insidious onset of shortness of breath. Clinically, they are differentiated from other causes of empyema in that they are not toxically ill but can have a high fever. These large pleural effusions are difficult to differentiate radiologically from other causes of a large effusion, as hilar adenopathy is seldom visible (Fig. 20). The effusion can vary in size from complete opacification of the whole hemithorax to a small effusion with only obliteration of the costophrenic angle. After draining the effusion, the enlarged glands or primary focus may become visible.

The diagnosis of TB pleural effusion is made by combining the clinical and radiological pictures. The diagnosis can be further substantiated by doing a diagnostic tap of the effusion. TB pleural effusion is characterized by the predominance of lymphocytes in the fluid. In younger children, the effusion is usually part of complicated lung disease. The pleural effusion is normally an inconsequential part of miliary TB, or lobar or bronchopneumonic tuberculosis (Fig. 21). In nearly all cases the TB effusion clears up rapidly on treatment. After three to four weeks of treatment, the pleural effusion will have cleared, with only slight pleural thickening still present.

Tuberculosis is the most common cause for a large pleural effusion in an adolescent patient.

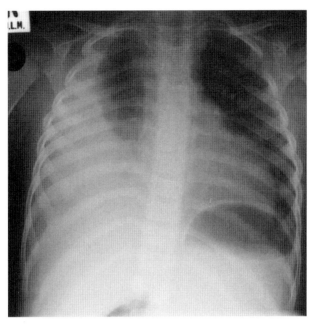

Figure 20. Uncomplicated right sided pleural effusion with no other radio-logical signs of primary TB visible.

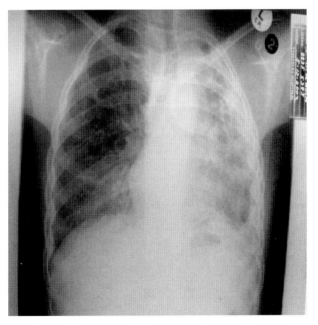

Figure 21. Small pleural effusion on the left-hand side, which is present with complicated underlying lung disease. The underlying lung disease is complicated by fibrosis, volume loss, and bilateral cavities.

VIII. MILIARY TUBERCULOSIS

Dissemination of a large number of organisms into the blood circulation follows the involvement of blood vessels by the primary complex. These large numbers of bacilli are then spread throughout the body and lead to the development of granulomas in all the involved organs. These children are clinically very ill and often have accompanying TB meningitis. As the granulomas are all similar in size, they are seen on chest radiographs as evenly distributed, small, millet-sized (less than 2 mm), round opacities (Fig. 22). They are often best observed on the lateral chest radiograph in the lower lobes.

If untreated, the nodules get larger as the disease progresses, and they can be difficult to differentiate from broncho-pneumonic opacification. The radiological picture of miliary TB can occur without any other classical radiological signs of primary TB being visible.

The disease most difficult to distinguish from miliary TB is lymphocytic interstitial pneumonia (LIP) in an HIV-infected child (see p. 42). If there is accompanying central nervous system involvement, the most likely diagnosis is miliary TB

Miliary TB is often accompanied by TB meningitis.

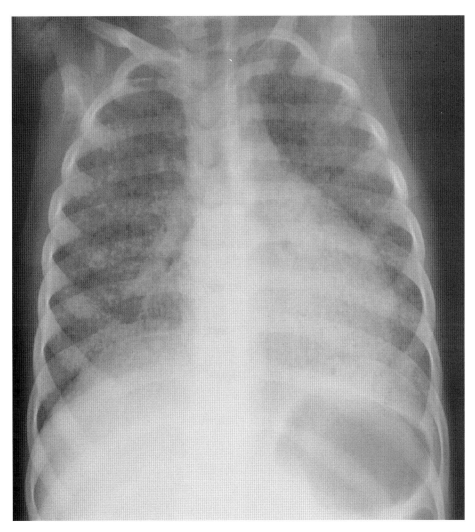

Figure 22. Fine millet-sized nodules typically seen in miliary TB. The nodules are all of similar size and spread through all the lung fields. No other radiological signs of primary TB are visible.

IX. POST-PRIMARY TUBERCULOSIS

Post-primary TB (adult-type) is seldom seen prior to adolescence. It occurs earlier in girls than it does in boys and presents with the same clinical and radiological picture as TB in adult patients.

The involvement, as in adults, is usually in the upper lobes or the apices of the lower lobes. Early in the course of the disease, there is vague opacification in the upper lobes which has been termed "smudge or cotton wool lesions". As the disease progresses, the lesions become more dense and eventually develop cavities (Figs. 23 and 24). The cavities, typically in the upper lobes, allow the spread of the TB to other parts of the lungs. The infection heals by fibrosis, leading to fibrotic upper lobes.

The approach to these adolescents is the same as the approach to an adult with suspected pulmonary TB. In adolescents, sputum microscopy remains the examination of choice in diagnosing TB.

> **Adolescents develop post-primary TB (adult-type TB), which in most cases is diagnosed by sputum smear microscopy**

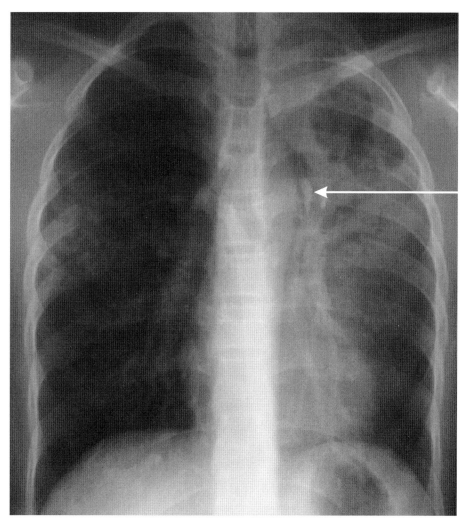

Figure 23. A case of post-primary tuberculosis in a 10-year-old boy who, until recently, had a normal chest radiograph. Cavities are present in the left upper lobe. This patient was sputum smear positive. Arrow indicates calcified lymph node due to previous primary infection.

Congenital and neonatal tuberculosis

With the increasing HIV epidemic, the number of infants presenting with congenital or neonatal TB is increasing.

The infant can be infected *in utero* and, in these cases, the emphasis is on the liver and the *porta hepatis* involvement. These infants have enlarged livers and non-specific lung disease. On the other hand, the neonate can be infected during the birth process by aspiration of infected material, or, shortly after birth, when the child is in contact with a diseased adult. The adult source case could be the mother, but it could also be any other household member.

Neonates infected shortly after birth develop broncho-pneumonia, which is very non-specific; hilar or mediastinal lymph node enlargement is often not seen (Fig. 24). In infants, gland compression of the airways is common, with 48% having compression of either the trachea or bronchi.

> **TB is often best diagnosed in infants and young children by examining the sputum and the chest radiograph of the mother or caregiver.**

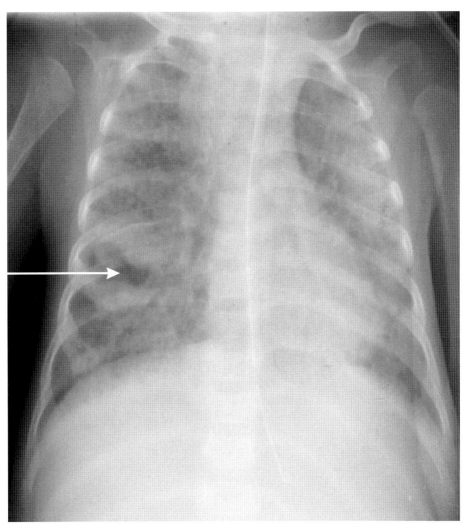

Figure 24. A 2-month-old infant with severe bilateral bronchopneumonia and a cavity in the right middle lobe (see arrow).

TB pericardial effusion
Although not a common form of TB, pericardial effusion can be suspected from examining the chest radiographs. TB pericardial effusion is present in less than 1% of children with TB. They present with an insidious onset of shortness of breath and signs of congestive cardiac failure. The radiographic picture of the chest is that of a large water bottle shaped heart and visible signs of congestive cardiac failure (Fig. 25).

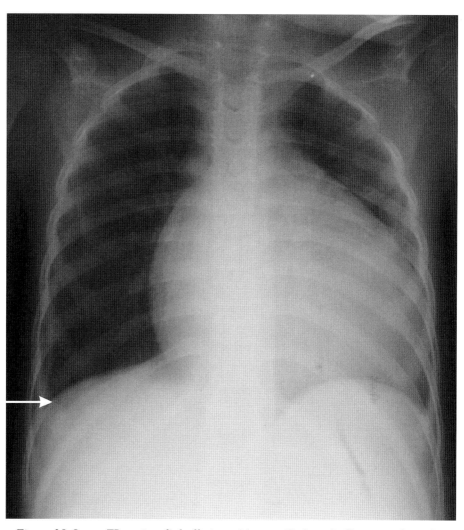

Figure 25. Large TB pericardial effusion with a small pleural effusion on the right-hand side, indicated by the arrow.

TB spondylitis (spinal TB)
Very seldom is unsuspected spinal TB diagnosed from the chest radiograph.
If the chest form has an unusual shape that is not due to technical factors,
examine the vertebrae carefully, as anterior collapse of the vertebrae leading
to gibbus formation can sometimes be seen (Figs. 26 and 27).

Phrenic nerve palsy and infiltration of other structures
Phrenic nerve palsy, chylothorax, and Horner syndrome can occur due to
infiltration of the various structures by TB.

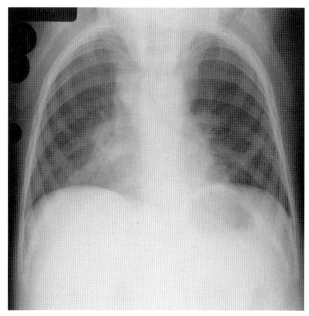

Figure 26. Spinal TB causes unusually shaped chest with opacification of the right middle lobe and lingula. The collapsed vertebrae are not visible on this view

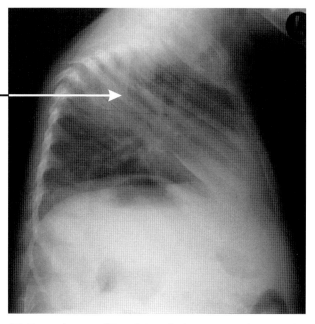

Figure 27. Lateral view of Fig. 26, with the arrow indicating the gibbus.

XI. HIV-INFECTED CHILDREN AND TUBERCULOSIS

When dealing with children infected with HIV, the diagnosis of TB is made even more difficult for a number of reasons:

1. HIV-related lung diseases share many of the clinical and radiological features associated with TB.

2. Tuberculin skin tests are more often non-reactive in HIV-infected children

3. The immune suppression caused by HIV leads to unusual forms of TB.

Miliary TB and lymphocytic interstitial pneumonia (LIP)

Children infected with HIV can develop chronic lung diseases that are difficult to distinguish from TB. One of the most difficult is LIP, which can closely resemble miliary TB on a chest radiograph. The matter is further complicated by the fact that both diseases can lead to hilar lymph gland enlargement, hepatosplenomegaly, and enlarged peripheral lymph glands.

These clinical factors help distinguish miliary TB from LIP:

1. LIP seldom occurs in children younger than one year, and usually starts in the second year of life.

2. Miliary TB is seldom associated with clubbing of the fingers and toes, while this occurs in most cases of LIP.

3. Parotid enlargement seldom occurs in miliary TB, while it is present in some cases of LIP.

4. Most children with miliary TB are acutely ill, with central nervous system involvement, while children with LIP are often not ill at all.

The following chest radiographic features are useful in distinguishing miliary TB from LIP (Fig. 28).

1. Miliary TB has widespread distribution of evenly-sized, small (< 2 mm) nodules.

2. In LIP, the nodules are larger and not uniform in size, with an accompanying reticular pattern.

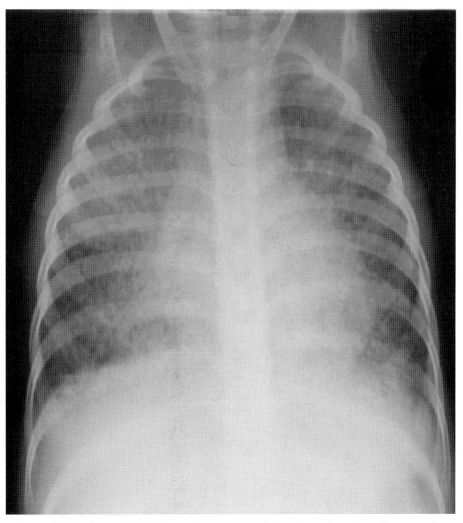

Figure 28. Patient with LIP. Note the coarse nodules of varying sizes. Compare this picture to the typical miliary TB picture (see Fig. 22).

In some cases, it is impossible to distinguish between miliary TB and LIP. These children are best treated for TB; if they respond, they probably had miliary TB, and, if the pattern remains unchanged, they probably have LIP.

The diagnosis can be further complicated by the HIV patient having LIP, and then becoming infected with TB and developing tuberculosis (Fig. 29).

Other diagnoses that can be confused with tuberculosis
Bronchiectasis secondary to pneumonia, tuberculosis, or LIP can cause chronic radiological changes that can be difficult to distinguish from TB. These bronchiectatic regions of the lung can also be the source of continued tuberculous disease requiring prolonged therapy.

Kaposi sarcomata occur in HIV-infected children who present with bloody pleural effusions or vague areas of consolidation in the lung fields. Often, the diagnosis is made or suspected by the additional presence of cutaneous, mucus membrane, or palate sarcomata.

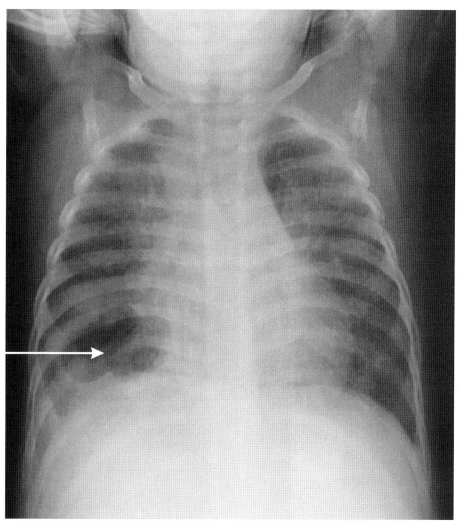

Figure 29. A patient with LIP who has developed a cavity in the right lower lobe due to concomitant infection with TB. Arrow indicates the cavity. Note the background coarse reticulo-nodular pattern caused by LIP.

Tuberculosis in HIV-infected children

HIV-infected children are more susceptible to TB than uninfected children. After being infected with *Mycobacterium tuberculosis,* HIV-infected children progress more rapidly to disease than do uninfected children. The clinical picture of tuberculosis in HIV-infected children is similar to that in uninfected children. The occurrence of miliary TB, pleural effusions, cavities, and massive TB glands is more common in HIV-infected children when compared to uninfected children (Fig. 30). The massive glands can be confused with lymphoma of the mediastinum.

> **In children, HIV-related lung disease is often confused with lung disease caused by TB.**

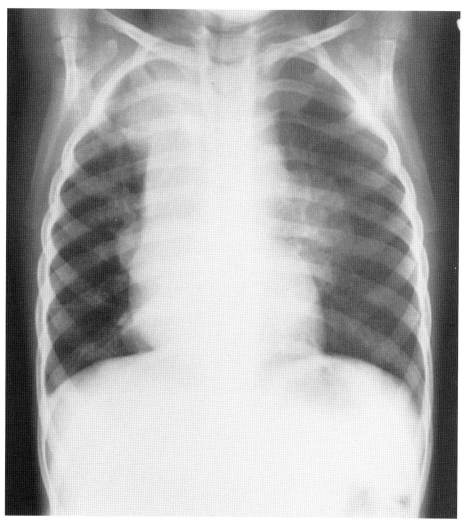

Figure 30. Patient dually infected with HIV and TB. Note the massive hilar and paratracheal glands caused by the TB.

XII. RESOLUTION OF CHEST RADIOGRAPHY ABNORMALITIES

It is commonly assumed that chest radiography changes disappear during therapy. In a small number of cases, the radiological picture can actually worsen after the start of treatment (Figs. 31, 32). In most of these cases, the patient remains asymptomatic, and, as treatment is continued, the radiographic picture improves. By the end of treatment for TB mediastinal lymph gland enlargement, approximately 66% of chest radiographs will be normal. After treatment, there can be continued improvement of the chest radiograph. Calcifications usually appear 12-18 months after treatment, but do occur earlier in younger children. These calcifications can occur in both parenchymal lesions and lymph nodes (see Fig. 12, p. 21).

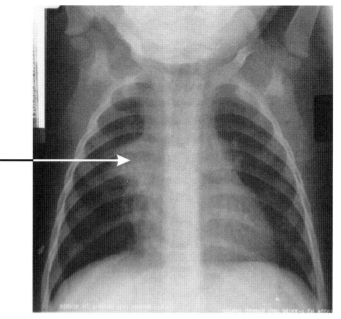

Figure 31. Patient with hilar lymph gland enlargement and infiltration of surrounding lung tissue (see arrow).

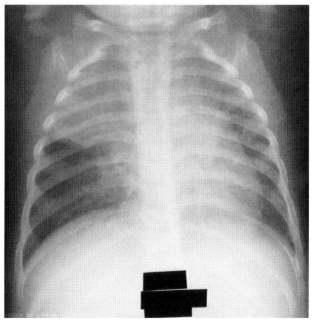

Figure 32. The chest radiograph of the same patient after 3 months of treatment, showing worsening picture due to occlusion of the right upper lobe bronchus. The patient's chest radiograph was normal after 6 months of treatment.

It can be extremely difficult to determine what the final outcome of the lung lesions will be at the start of treatment. Treatment of extensive lesions can lead to remarkable improvement due to fibrosis of the lesions (Figs. 33, 34).

> **Do not predict what the final outcome will be at the beginning of treatment.**

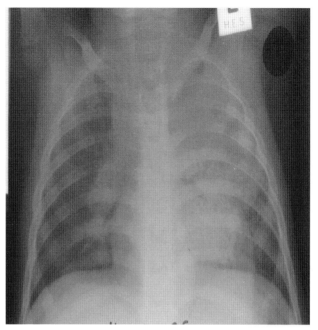

Figure 33. Patient with extensive consolidation and a cavity in the left upper lobe, with accompanying right hilar and paratracheal lymph gland enlargement.

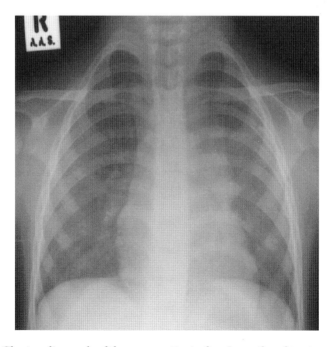

Figure 34. Chest radiograph of the same patient after 6 months of treatment, showing only fibrosis of the left upper lobe.

XIII. LONG-TERM CONSEQUENCES OF INTRATHORACIC TUBERCULOSIS

In a small percentage of cases, children who have had extensive TB have long-term damage of their lungs and airways. The incidence of long-term damage in children co-infected with HIV-TB still needs to be determined, but it seems to be higher than in children uninfected with HIV.

The most common long-term consequence is an area of lung fibrosis. These areas are of little consequence, as the children remain asymptomatic.

The most troublesome long-term consequence is bronchiectasis (Fig 35). Children with bronchiectasis of the lower lobes remain symptomatic, with repeated respiratory tract infections and continued production of purulent sputum. They often get misdiagnosed as having a recurrence of their TB and get re-treated or treated more than once for TB. These patients often require a lobectomy to resolve their symptoms. Bronchiectasis of the upper lobes is more often asymptomatic and requires less attention.

Bronchiectasis of the lower lobes is the most troublesome long-term consequence of primary TB.

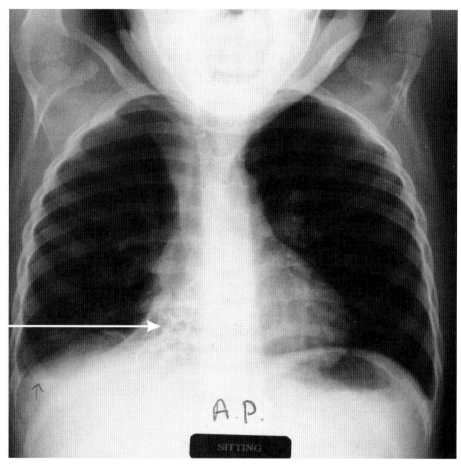

Figure 35. The cystic (honeycombing) changes characteristic of bronchiectasis can be seen in the right middle and lower lobes. The arrow indicates the cystic changes.

XIV. THE IMPORTANT FACTS ABOUT CHILDHOOD TB FOR LOW-INCOME COUNTRIES

1. TB can occur at any age. The highest burden of disease is found among children less than 4 years of age, with the highest burden found in children younger than 1 year.

2. Adult, smear-positive index cases are 10 times more infective than smear-negative index cases.

3. About 50% of children exposed to adult index cases will become infected.

4. The younger the child the greater the risk of developing disease, with 40% of children under 1 year, 30% of children under 4 years, and 15% of infected adolescents developing disease.

5. Children attending school (6-14 years of age) have the lowest incidence of disease (golden school-going age).

6. The two most serious forms of TB are acute disseminated TB and TB meningitis, with the highest incidence in young children, especially those less than 2-years of age.

7. A positive tuberculin skin test means infection with TB, not TB disease or immunity to TB.

8. Children develop paucibacillary TB (few organisms). This is important, as children are less likely to have smear-positive TB, can be treated with fewer drugs, and are less likely to develop multidrug-resistant TB (MDR TB).

9. The chest radiograph picture in children is the result of mediastinal lymph gland enlargement and the complications of the lymph gland enlargement.

10. Children are treated by DOTS.

11. MDR TB is as infective as drug-sensitive TB. MDR TB in children is suspected if the adult index case is not responding to treatment, or is being retreated for TB.

12. Chemoprophylaxis and treatment of latent infection is important in young children (< 2 years) as they have the highest chance of developing serious disease (Miliary TB and TB meningitis).

13. Children infected with HIV have the greatest risk of developing TB disease. There should be a high degree of suspicion that HIV-infected children have developed TB. An HIV-infected child in contact with an adult index case requires thorough investigation and either treatment or chemoprophylaxis for TB.

14 In children infected with both TB and HIV, the diagnosis is more difficult. HIV-related lung disease has similar symptoms; the children are less likely to have a positive tuberculin skin test; and the radiological pictures may be confused with TB (LIP).

15. TB in HIV-infected children is treated the same way as TB in children not infected with HIV.

16. Adolescents develop either TB pleural effusion or post-primary TB (adult-type) and are examined and treated in the same way as adult TB patients with similar disease.